11 Steps to
Turn your
Garden Japanese

(without spending a fortune or taking years to see results!)

Russell Chard

Copyright © 2013 by Zenibo Publishing

All rights reserved. No part of this book may be reproduced in any form or by any electronic or mechanical means including information storage and retrieval systems – except in the case of brief quotations in articles or reviews – without the permission in writing from its publisher, Zenibo Publishing

All brand names and product names used in this book are trademarks, registered trademarks, or trade names of their respective holders. We are not associated with any product or vendor in this book.

Related websites:
www.makingajapanesegarden.com
www.japzen.wordpress.com
www.japzengardens.org

 facebook.com/japanesegardens

 @japangdninfo

Contents

Introduction	4
Japanese Gardens - Explained	8
Japanese Garden History	10
Japanese Gardens – Basic Design Principles	18
Important Questions to Answer Before Starting to Turn Your Japanese Garden	24
The 11 Simple Ways to Turn Your Garden Japanese	31
A Japanese Oasis	77

INTRODUCTION

Hi,

Thank you for buying my book '11 Simple Ways To Turn Your Garden Japanese'

My aim in creating this book is to inspire you and give you lots of useful ideas to add a 'touch' of Japan to your yard or garden.

First off, let me give you some background...

My name is Russ Chard - this is me

-and, I've written about Japanese gardens for many years and my interest started after a visit to one of North America's finest Japanese gardens in San Francisco and has developed into a fully-grown passion of mine. I am grateful that my flight back to London was delayed that day and I chose a garden visit rather than sitting in the airport for 7 hours!

Pathways, Stepping Stones, Manicured Trees and Shrubs, Raked Gravel with Island and Dwarf Bonsai Tree – San Francisco's Japanese Garden

Since then I have created and run several websites on Japanese gardens and they are read by people from all over the world on a daily basis. They cover all aspects of Japanese and Zen gardens (sometimes known as Japanese Rock gardens). Here are details of my websites:

www.japzen.wordpress.com

www.makingajapanesegarden.com

www.whatisazengarden.com

I have a Twitter feed @japangdninfo and a Facebook page: www.facebook.com/zenibo777 and have even set up an online Japanese garden magazine that I update daily from wherever I happen to be! Such is the beauty of technology.

It is that same technology that allows you to access my latest book literally in seconds and I am very glad to be able to share these ideas with you.

I have also enlisted the help of a Japanese garden designer friend of mine called Tim Sykes. Years ago he decided to de-stress and give up the rat race of working in advertising and trained in Horticultural Design. Together with his wife, Tim has run a very successful bespoke garden design company for nearly 10 years and he loves Japanese gardens!

I have written this book because experience has taught me that the idea of having a full-blown Japanese garden at a home or in a workspace is unworkable for many people let alone impractical.

Japanese gardens are beautiful, peaceful, simple, steeped in history and meaning and large ones cannot be constructed cheaply or without dedication - not only for their construction but for their on-going maintenance as well.

To have a fairly large Japanese garden is a BIG commitment. After all, the reason they look so striking and unique is because of the planning and care and attention that goes into them.

If you have unlimited funds and time on your hands then your Japanese garden project will be easy and the sky is the limit. But, as you and I know the vast majority of people do not fall into this category and so money and time are important.

You cannot build a Japanese garden in a weekend from scratch nor can you learn how to build one in 3 minutes as a video I saw recently on YouTube claimed!

But here's some GOOD news...

You don't have to be restricted by the obstacles you may perceive that I have laid before you. With a little know how adding a touch of Japan to your garden or home is very achievable and this book will give you 11 ways of doing exactly that.

You won't have to break the bank to do it nor will they be unreasonably time consuming to create. Your Japanese garden will be on a smaller scale than some you have seen but NO LESS memorable!

Along with top Japanese garden designer Tim Sykes, I have come up with a book that we believe will explain in plain English the basics of Japanese gardens and how with that new found knowledge you can set about transforming a space at your home that will be eye catching, soothing for the soul and the envy of your family and friends too!

You don't need to spend a fortune on garden designers either as Tim and I will be teaching you the finer points of Japanese gardening and showing you practical ways where sometimes doing very little will give you the style of garden or area that you desire.

An important principle to understand is that Japanese

gardens are nature in miniature and that is why they appear balanced and harmonious. Mimicking nature to a Japanese garden designer can be as simple as taking in a vista and copying the landscape from memory or a picture only on a much smaller scale.

This is EXACTLY why these types of gardens work in modest spaces and don't have to be large and complicated.

Get ready to be inspired by our words, design plans, ideas and simple instructions that will demystify the subject of Japanese gardens and set you well on the way to adding a Japanese flavour to your garden, yard, balcony, courtyard, hallway or wherever you have the available space!

Read on....

>   **RUSSELL CHARD**
>   **EDITOR**

www.turnyourgardenjapanese.com

Email: zeniboltd@aol.com

Japanese Gardens - Explained

What you REALLY need to know to easily have a beautiful, serene garden area for relaxation and contemplation just like the Japanese do!

Japanese gardens are growing in popularity around the globe. North America has over 250 that are open to the public. Europe has some fine examples as does Australasia. People from all over the world appreciate the beauty of a Japanese garden as soon as they set foot in one.

Visitors are struck by their appearance, ingredients, manicured trees and shrubs, rock formations, bridges, Tea houses, water features, lanterns , meandering pathways, viewing areas, religious meaning, serenity, history, gates, fencing, colours in the fall, koi ponds and perhaps most notable of all that feeling of stepping into another world away from the stresses and strains of the day.

The history of Japanese gardens stretches back hundreds of years. When Japan started trading with China it was natural that cultural exchanges would take place and perhaps strangely to some people - gardening was an important part of the relationship between the Chinese and Japanese.

Japanese traders and high-ranking officials including priests absorbed Chinese culture and that influence can be seen in Japanese art and gardens today. To the Japanese - gardens are living works of art. They are status symbols too and even today some of Japan's finest private examples remain closed to the public.

As time went by Japanese gardens became less exclusive and often were built in the simplest of ways at domestic residences. It is these smaller gardens that will provide our inspiration as well as your understanding of the design and development of larger more complicated gardens and their significance in your garden ideas and project.

Just by adding some stones or rocks along with some plants and shrubs you can quickly have a garden area with a Japanese feel. You can add ornaments or bridges, bamboo fencing, trees, water features, pathways, basins, deer-scarers in fact there is a long list of ingredients that will help you achieve your goal of an eye catching, calm space with the authenticity you desire.

With a little imagination and effort your garden will be the envy of your family and friends and they WILL want to know how you did it!

You can have an indoor garden too or one on a balcony or between two buildings in an unused space ,I am sure that you have had an eye on a space in your yard or garden to potentially turn Japanese and that is one of the reasons you wanted to read this book: to get some help and inspiration.

First off let's take a little trip into the history of Japanese gardens which will give you a very good indication as to why some of the ingredients we associate with a Japanese garden are still very relevant in modern Japanese gardens.

Japanese Garden History

Because the history of Japanese garden stretches back hundreds of years, it is a fairly complicated subject. For the purpose of this book it is practical to give you a 'potted history' so that you can begin to absorb and understand their meaning, development and their relevance today in modern Japanese gardens.

As far back as the early part of the first millennia the Chinese started designing recreational gardens and as they developed news of these structures and their ingredients spread.

Gardening was almost a philosophy and it's fair to say reached its peak in ancient times in Japan. The Japanese started off by creating a sort of *'light'* version of Chinese gardens, for want of a better term they distilled what the Chinese had done to suit their own culture and beliefs.

So, the Japanese imported these garden ideas from China during the period known as the Han Dynasty.

The Emperor Wu Di who lived from **140-87 BC** first created a garden containing 3 small islands. These represented the Isles of the Immortals who were considered to be Taoist gods and this garden set a trend for ALL gardens to solely concentrate on replicating the land of legend.

Today Japanese gardens mimic nature but this was not the case during the Han period and the only gardens designed and constructed were ones of mythical lands and landscapes meaning religious beliefs and good old fashioned imagination worked in tandem.

The first hill and pond garden in Japan was established in the early 600's AD when the Chinese Emperor Yang Di enjoyed relations with Japan at his instigation.

The Japanese responded to these overtures and sent an envoy to China who was a man called Ono no Imoko. He became immersed in China and its culture and met with the emperor on many occasions.

Upon his return to Japan he took with him much of what he had learnt and the art of gardening was just one facet of Chinese culture he was keen to relate to the Japanese people. Another idea imported to Japan around the same time was Buddhism.

The Shinto Tradition: Asuka era 552 – 646 AD

During this period the appreciation of the Shinto belief started to take a small hold in Japan. The Shinto religion looked upon nature as a god (s) - certain types of rocks and trees were openly worshipped.

A rice straw rope was used to seal off the 'deity' rock or large stone which pronounced the area as a holy piece of land where nature and man were at one. This was the essence of a Japanese garden during this period.

The word *Niwa* in Japanese means a cultivated field but it was also a term that was used to refer to a holy piece of land around a stone or a tree.

The Nara Era- 646-794AD

This was really the time in Japanese history that Chinese ideology started to blend in with Japanese life and traditions.

In fact, the word *Niwa* first appeared in the Japanese language during this period, previously it was a Chinese expression for the type of holy sites mentioned previously.

The garden architecture of this period used walkways- often

between buildings and they also used stones and shrubs to actually compliment the buildings themselves. More often than not, the buildings were Royal palaces or shrines and temples.

These types of gardens are known as *Shinden.* Buddhism and it's teachings became commonplace during this period and something called *Shumisen* became increasingly popular – in short this is a Buddhist representation of the centre of the universe.

Gardens would have a central large stone that represented the home of the Buddha and it would be surrounded by a collection of smaller stones that would indicate the Buddha's disciples.

THE HEIAN ERA

This period ran from 794 to 1185AD and is generally accepted as being the period of opulence and luxury in Japan. Elegance was the watchword of the day.

Japanese gardens developed into much larger and wealthy creations and were usually the domain of the rich and the famous. They were status symbols and it was a requirement of the rich to understand and practise good garden design and follow the clear and developing rules.

The **Heian** period had its own garden fashion mostly made up of viewing gardens and the introduction of water features such as ponds which encouraged the gardens owners to make use of their boats!

It is during this period of Japanese history that the first signs of what we now know as modern Japanese gardening first appeared. *Tachibana no Toshitsuna* wrote the book of garden or *Sakuteiki*, which today is seen as the starting point of Japanese gardening.

Its importance to Japanese gardening cannot be underestimated as this early book freed designers from the constraints of Chinese influenced gardening in Japan. The Chinese based nearly all their garden design on *feng shui*. This only allowed certain features to be constructed in a specific way as well encouraging placement with perfect geometry.

The *Sakuteiki* threw the Chinese rule book out of the window and recommended amongst other things that the Japanese garden designer should use the placement of stones as a priority. A significant and major departure from what had been before.

Heian period gardens are known in Japanese as *Chisen Shuyu Teien* ,in English this translates as 'Pond-spring boating gardens'.Water ,usually in the form of a pond was at the epicentre of the garden and there is a specific type of way to view this garden....from the water!

Owners would love to show off these types of gardens and guests would view from beautifully crafted wooden boats to the strains of an orchestra. Impressive and eye catching at the same time.

THE KAMAKURA ERA- 1185-1392

This was the period of even greater change in Japanese garden design.

The garden was seen as a perfect place for reflection and contemplation. They are the gardens that had a *Zen* influence due to the new Shogun and his Samurai embracing *Zen* as their religion.

This meant that in the Japanese garden recreation was no longer considered appropriate and mediation and reflection were. Garden designers were either priests or very religious people.

Muso Soseki was the leading Japanese garden designer during the **Kamakura** era. He lived from 1275 to 1351AD. His principle design idea for a garden made the visitor actually walk around the garden to view it correctly from many different angles as opposed to sitting in a boat or looking from a building (one angle)

The idea was that the visitor would appreciate and think about the changing views as they walked around the garden – today these gardens in English are referred to a Strolling gardens or Viewing gardens.

Soseki was the forefather of something referred to as *'borrowed scenery'* and the idea of 'hide and reveal' meaning seeing something from one viewing angle that you would not necessarily be able to see from another. Surprise and intrigue was the objective.

These design principles remain an integral part of many Japanese garden designs to this day.

Religion and its indelible link to Japanese gardens is a common thread throughout much of Japanese history. Priests were known as *Ishitateso* or in English 'rock setting priests'- not exactly a glamorous title because these priests were in effect 'juniors' – elders and more senior religious figures would consider such work as beneath them.

Over time these religious 'manual workers' who started out simply looking for appropriate rocks for gardens across Japan, suddenly through their expertise and dedication to their cause became revered and by the early 15th century they enjoyed a much more important status through their skill and craft.

The Zen Influence in Japanese Gardens

Japan has a period of civil wars in the **Muromachi** period-

1393 to 1558AD and it was a time of significant unrest. Life carried on even in the face of adversity and this period gave rise to the *Tea Ceremony* as well as other significant cultural changes.

In gardening the emergence of the *Kare sansui* or 'Dry landscape garden' happened in this period. They were simple gardens but full of meaning and demonstrated a Zen influence. Their simplicity was striking and they consisted of stones, rocks and gravel (or sand).

War brought with it suffering and a shortage of water. Dry landscape gardens therefore became the norm because they needed no watering.

Their simplicity meant that it was now not just the rich who could have a garden.

Karesansui gardens had no human interference and were not designed to be walked through as these gardens were artistic statements and viewed as living art in the form of a natural painting.

They were the forerunners of the *'Zen gardens'* that you see today also sometimes referred to as Japanese rock gardens.

Notably, the *Japanese courtyard garden* was built in often less ornate and smaller homes and was designed to be a centrepiece once inside the dwelling with a specific viewing area being set aside for contemplation and relaxation.

As time passed Japanese gardens became even more elaborate - using bridges, cut stone pathways, trees, ornaments and alike.

A new type of Japanese garden was soon to become very socially acceptable – the Tea garden. Monks and priests took Tea to keep themselves alert and the Tea garden began to flourish during the period **Momoyama** period 1568-1600 AD. The Tea ceremony was a highly significant religious tradition and Tea gardens began to spring up in some of Japan's most influential areas.

Kyoto is the spiritual home of the Japanese garden and it used to be the centre of the Japanese empire. Some of Japan's finest examples of Tea gardens can be found in this area. *Konchi-in* is one and features a small temple within a much larger monastery called *Nanzen-ji*.

Because of the emerging significance of the Tea garden Japan's leading Tea Master was called *Sen no Rikyu* and he lead the call in the *Momoyama* period for much more rustic gardens to be the place where Tea ceremony could be undertaken.

Out went the lavish and ornate and in came an almost peasant feel to the garden and its ingredients and his own garden was very basic. The Tea garden has an entrance and a pathway that stretches through the garden before reaching the Tea house where the ceremony would take place. Visitors were encouraged to take in the gardens simple and natural beauty before attending the ceremony.

Zen gardens on the other hand were first off just simple gardens before later becoming synonymous with meditation and reflection.

Japanese Gardens-1603 to 1867AD

This 254 year period was known as the **Edo period**, Japan was getting richer through expansion and trade and as the population became wealthier they needed something to spend their money on. On cue a new popular career path emerged -Japanese garden designers - who were satisfying a significant nationwide demand and springing up all over the country.

Designers and house and land owners used the established ideas of centuries of Japanese gardening but no real new styles emerged. Gardens and their ingredients and look were at the whim of the owner but maintaining historical accuracies.

Combination gardens were common featuring lots of different ideas and designs. The art of Japanese gardening stayed true to itself but unavoidably as the world started to get a little smaller some foreign ideas began to slowly creep into some gardens.

However, of all the types of gardening in the world it is the Japanese who have a traceable history and a reverence to their forefathers and ideas.

JAPANESE GARDENS – BASIC DESIGN PRINCIPLES

The simplest way to achieve your dream Japanese garden with clarity and understanding so that you can have a future of relaxation, serenity and visually stunning beauty

In Western garden design most areas of the garden tend to be quite strictly designed. In a Japanese garden a little improvisation is preferred and if you are working from a design allow yourself to change the plan if it looks and feels right.

A Western garden is admired for its construction, colours and plantings.

A Japanese garden is about reproducing and symbolizing the outside world but making it look as though human involvement is not evident - it is disguised.

Western gardens are symmetrical whilst Japanese gardens are asymmetrical with plants and trees presented in a rustic or rugged way. Many types of Japanese gardens will have flowers, trees and fruits that reflect the seasons and the gardens natural relationship to the space that it is in.

The Japanese have a love affair with nature and it is natural that this passion has been reflected in their gardens for hundreds of years. Some of the earliest gardens discovered date back to the 7th century with mini mountains and bodies of water.

The Shinto Japanese religion teaches that the world and everything in it is influenced by nature's creative forces. The 'borrowing' of distant scenery into a Japanese garden demonstrates this homage to the forces of creation. This is called Shakkei in Japanese.

A golden rule of Japanese gardening is requiring the designer to sense what works and what looks good, so if you wish to copy a landscape that you like in a Japanese garden style, you will need to either have a good memory or make use of a camera or video recorder to capture the landscape that you wish to copy in miniature.

Japanese gardens require a quiet area as their essence is contemplation, reflection and even meditation. This serene feeling is a major factor in why so many people want to add a touch of Japan to their gardens or yards.

Reflecting reality is an important principle in a Japanese garden and a great example would be a 'Zen' style garden with its large raked areas of gravel which depict the sea or a body of water populated by a small number of rocks or larger stones that depict mountains and in some cases land mass like islands.

Japanese gardens NEVER try and create a feature that is not present within nature - a Western garden takes natural elements and rearranges them into unnatural structures or areas.

The most popular types of designs for domestic Japanese gardens are:

Zen gardens or Japanese rock gardens - The Zen Buddhist influence in this variety of garden makes them simple and perfect for meditation and contemplation. They are perfect for small to medium sized spaces and use sand and gravel to depict water, rocks and stones for mountains and islands with a minimum of greenery in the form of plants.

You can use plants on the edges of the 'dry water' space as long as they are varieties that you would find by a sea-shore. However, many people use other types of plants and shrubs and in a world of 'freewill' you can certainly do the same!

Tea Gardens - One of the most significant but sparse types of Japanese garden. They have an entrance, a pathway that leads through the garden space to a water basin for cleansing the hands and face ahead of the Tea ceremony. A Tea garden can have stone ornaments but only sparingly as it is the most austere of gardens.

A Tea garden has a 'tea house' or pavilion where the Tea ceremony is carried out. The significant feeling of this type of garden is one of quiet and calm.

Hill and Pond Gardens - as the name suggests both of those elements feature prominently. A hill or hills have a water body at the front of them. This can either be a pond or a 'dry water' area of either sand or gravel.

Hills must be in proportion with each other to give the garden its natural look and plants that can be used if you wish to achieve authenticity should be flowers, plants and shrubs that grow naturally in hilly areas.

Pathways can also be built to show off the hill and pond relationship within nature and as before around the water's edge should be plants that grow naturally in that environment.

You aim should be to create a quiet area of meditative ambience using your chosen style and ingredients. Never be afraid to have empty spaces as in Japanese gardens they should blend in with the finished design and will add to the gardens look and feel.

Water, Ornaments, Basins, Bridges, Paths and Why Size IS Everything!

Many Japanese gardens are designed to be viewed from a single place so the design is carefully done to show off the best features from this point including any scenery 'borrowing' that can be incorporated into the garden design.

For example, a hill or mountain may be visible from your garden and you may wish to use its distant view within your garden. a really effective way of doing this is to 'frame' the object with stones or plants. This is quite advanced Japanese garden design.

Japanese garden design treats water with reverence. Fountains are not natural so are uncommon in Japanese gardens. You may crave a fountain and there is no hard and fast rule that says that you cannot have one in your space!

Waterfalls are more common but achieve maximum effect in a large garden, they are popular in Japanese garden design as the movement of the water is natural, a recurring theme as I am sure you are noticing..

Water can also be used in low level streams that give off the sound of a rippling brook and also in water basins. Both of these features will require a well-disguised water pump. A Deer-scarer is another aquatic option but more about those later in this book. Water in a Japanese garden is required to be clean and pure.

Ornaments in Japanese gardens tend to be understated and on the small side. The garden has a beginning an end and larger stone sculptures will distract the visitor and viewer from the gardens purpose.

Lanterns, water basins, lions, stone bridges are all common ingredients but used sparingly. Natural rocks are utilised in small groupings - always odd numbers - and they have names too. The tall vertical stone, the low vertical stone, reclining stones and arched stones but don't get hung up on these specific shapes and meaningful stones as there are many shapes and sizes that you can use and source locally to where you live.

In Japan colour, shape, texture and even the grain of a rock or stone are important because a weathered rock or a smooth stone reflect images of nature.

Paths and bridges represent a journey not only through the garden but for the spirit of the visitor. Paths are either straight or feature right-angle corners as the Japanese believe that Demons cannot turn on right-angles. Paths can be made of lots of closely placed stones or made to look like a series of stepping stones. The latter is achieved by making the stones stick out slightly from the ground (approximately 1 inch or 2.5 centimetres) whilst being firmly secured - once again this is a natural look and not a manufactured one.

Bridges invariably pass over some sort of water and provide a place to stop and contemplate within the garden. They can be ornate and wooden or arched granite across either water or dry water.

Japanese gardens can be huge or very small and that is part of their attraction. The design principles are the same whatever the size. So, now you hopefully understand a lot more about the design elements of Japanese gardens let's get down to the exciting bit.

Everything in a Japanese garden is kept to a minimum and a really good design tip it to sketch a design that almost looks empty and just features a couple of elements. You can always add to a Japanese garden but taking ingredients away is costly and time consuming. Get a feel for your garden design once you have made it become a reality and you will really get a sense of any additions that you need to make.

Important Questions to Answer BEFORE Starting to Turn Your Garden Japanese

How much available space do you have?

This is one of the most important things to get right. You probably have an unused area in your yard or garden or maybe you have an eye on part of your existing garden that you would like to revamp? Either way you have to identify a space and start picturing in your mind's eye what you want it to look like.

Imagination based on established ideas goes a long way in Japanese gardening. If you want a small area then think miniature, if you want a larger garden area think 'bigger'.

Do not rush in to clearing an area or digging up what you already have - take your time to really think through the space and area that will be your tranquil and serene garden space.

Once you have really thought it through and decided on a space and what you want to achieve mark out the entire space with some string or garden wire and secure all of its sides. If your garden is going to be square or a rectangle shape then the string should show precisely where your garden is going to be and reflect its exact size.

This outline is the first part of your Japanese garden space and you will be able to really see it start to come alive. If you have some stones or rocks or perhaps an ornament like a Japanese lantern place them in the garden space where you think they will be permanently. Give it a few days and keep taking in your placements visually and from different angles.

Whatever feels right should LOOK right and you will instinctively know if your ingredients are in the correct place. Don't be afraid to move stuff around and back again to help you decide - it really helps.

Is your chosen space as secluded and quiet as possible?

Japanese gardens and in particular Zen gardens are meant to be as quiet as possible so even if you have an ideal space that is near a neighbour's property or close to a boundary that perhaps is next to a road or busy pathway then you probably need to reconsider your 'spaces' position.

Your touch of Japan at home needs to be as tranquil as possible to give the space you desire a soothing, gentle feeling and at one with nature. If you wish to build an indoor garden space like a courtyard garden or a corridor garden then try and apply the same principles to your design. Choose a quieter are inside your property.

Tranquillity is important and it may mean that you will have to rearrange your existing garden area to accommodate what you are trying to achieve BUT it will be worth it!

Have you sketched out an outline plan of your chosen garden space?

Don't be under the illusion that you need a degree in technical drawing to do this. Our garden designs start life as A4 pieces of paper with a rough scalable sketch. By this we mean our plan is laid out with a workable scale for example 2 inches to one foot , you can choose whatever scale you wish but the plan has to reflect the exact space that you have marked out as mentioned earlier. Include any features in your design such as ornaments, pathways, stones, rocks, bridges, gravel etc and play around with the 'paper' placements, move stuff around within your design and don't forget to do this in tandem with studying your marked out area. Obviously your first rough plan should be done in pencil so you can easily make amendments.

It is very satisfying to see your ideas on paper and brought to a conclusion before the construction begins. You will find this planning stage makes the building of your Japanese garden space MUCH easier. So, don't skip it.

What will you need to change about your current space?

You may have the perfect space that is being used for something else in your yard. Consider the work and the overall benefit to your finished space (both Japanese and non-Japanese) before making drastic landscaping decisions.

Clearing a desired plot for your new exciting project maybe the only answer and clearly this means more work and maybe a little more expense. The decision rests on how much you want a Japanese space in your garden and the amount of effort you are prepared to put in to realise your dream.

Avoid removing large trees, try not to change ,divert or remove natural water sources - you should be thinking of ways to use them for your project instead!

A good idea once you have marked out your chosen area is to flatten it as much as possible and give the area recognisable and definite 'edges'. What you take out in the way of plants and shrubs and flowers can be carefully repositioned and replanted away from your Japanese area.

What type of Japanese style garden area are you keen to develop?

A big decision. If you wish to have a Zen style garden then a flat area is essential. If you want a pathway with an entrance and plants and shrubs etc. then slight landscape undulations will make the space more authentic.

A pond garden is ambitious but a lot of people love water features and if constructed correctly with an area of hills behind the pond and the right plants and shrubs this type of Japanese garden can look stunning.

If your climate permits you may want a Bonsai area next to a Zen style dry garden? The great thing is you can mix and match styles next to each other providing you have enough space.

If you have a big space you have so many options as you do if you have a smaller space although the latter will probably mean that you will stick to one style of Japanese garden for your first project.

Cost is an aspect to give thought to. If money is no object then you can achieve whatever you want to. This book is about helping you have a wonderfully relaxing Japanese garden space that is not going to break the bank whether small or a little larger - and it can be done!

Will you be ambitious and do-it-yourself or will you enlist the help of a professional?

Confidence and budget is all the answer to this questions boils down to. A professional will drain your budget and rightly so.

Small space Japanese style gardens can be constructed with the minimum of fuss. Your task could be a lot easier on this front if you only intend to have a tiny area with a few stones, gravel and perhaps an ornament.

Plantings need to be climate friendly and this book will give you plenty of help. Garden centres have experts that offer advice for free and you will have an aggregate merchant near your home for many ingredients that you will need.

Edging for example is something that has to be done correctly so a local builder or maybe a friend could help you out with 'pointing' (the permanent joining of granite blocks with cement for your gardens boundaries} for example.

The important thing about the construction process is that if you make a mistake or it does not look right you will be able to rectify the problem fairly easily by yourself. A good plan and layout should mean that this should not happen!

If you require large stones for your area they will need to be delivered and transferred into your garden space - make sure that you have an area where the equipment to do this heavy lifting work can get access.

The bigger the garden space the more help you will need from professionals because realistically you will have neither the time nor the desire to take on such a big ambitious project on your own.

For quick and very striking results our advice is think smaller - it's practical and will get your confidence up for expanding your Japanese style area in the future or adding more areas over time.

What ingredients are you interested in having?

There are many to choose from and perhaps you already have some clear ideas. For the ambitious there are Tea houses, ponds, large rocks and stones, Bridges etc. For smaller Japanese style gardens there are stone basins, a deerscarer, smaller rocks and stones, pathways, plants and shrubs, Bamboo fencing, water features, sand and gravel, trees and so on.

You need to pick ingredients that are in keeping with your design and remember cluttering is not an option! A Japanese style garden or space should be 'clean and ordered' to look at and not overwhelming to the eye.

Think carefully about what you would like and where it would be placed. Some ingredients will take more time to incorporate into your ideas others are comparatively simple.

This book will give you 11 simple ideas to turn your garden Japanese and they will not break the bank either.

Have you done a little research?

Research is important, you will get lots of inspirational ideas and tips from this book as well as a good basic background in Japanese garden design. Like any subject it is more complicated but this book is designed to keep it simple.

Our websites will give you lots more information on all aspects of Japanese gardens and you can visit them here:

http://www.japzen.wordpress.com

http://www.makingajapanesegarden.com

http://www.whatisazengarden.com

Tim's landscaping website is
http://www.reallygardenproud.com

ALL of them have invaluable ideas, videos, articles and lots of advice and tips.

What is your reason/concept for adding a Japanese style to your garden?

Is your garden space simply to look at? Is it for relaxation? Perhaps it has been a long standing dream and ambition of yours to change an area of your garden to one with a Japanese style? Have you been inspired on a visit to a Japanese or Zen garden and thought to yourself 'I would love something like that at my home'? You may be keen to copy a landscape that you have seen?

Whatever your reason it is important to have one because that will be the driving force for your project from start to finish.

Take the bull by the horns and promise yourself that once you start you WILL finish your garden space otherwise there is no point in starting. You will really feel as though you are accomplishing something as you go through the various stages of design and construction.

I did at my home as you can see below – a small space Zen garden in a suitable area that is soothing to look at and calming. Be determined, fluid in your thoughts and maybe even set yourself a deadline to get your garden finished!

BEFORE

Space was identified, marked out as a plot, rock placement to check the positioning and then the work could begin.

AFTER

Note the 3 rocks placed together, and a small grass island in the foreground with a smaller rock near its centre to indicate an island within the sea (the sand)

The 11 Simple Ways to Turn Your Garden Japanese

You want your dream Japanese garden space to look good, not break the bank and provide you with a calming space to relax in and generally feel good about life.

You will get pleasure from the beauty around you and have a garden space that you should feel you deserve to spend time in. It could be a tiny indoor or outdoor space with just 2 rocks placed in an enclosed space known in Japanese as a *tsuboniwa* or a larger area where you can let your thoughts and imagination be together as one.

Imagine a place of privacy and rest that encompasses the sounds of nature like trickling water plus soft textures, plants, candle light, scents, stones and rocks, wind chimes and all four elements of life.

We have come up with 11 SIMPLE ways to add a Japanese feel to your chosen space and you can combine ideas or just pick one theme or idea and stick to that.

As you will see you can easily combine ingredients but remember don't over clutter your space. The whole idea is for you to be able to build an area that feels Japanese whilst not altering your total yard or garden space merely complimenting it.

So, let's started with inspiring you to get going.

1) Pathways

Pathways in a Japanese garden have a beginning and an end. For example in a Tea garden the pathway would start at a specific entrance point and lead to the Tea house where ceremonial activities take place. Paths are journeys rather like our journey through life from beginning to end.

Japanese garden paths are nearly always straight and if they 'turn' they do so at right-angles as the Japanese believe that demons cannot travel easily on non-curved paths.

You can have a very attractive pathway within your garden that can be partially sunken stones within a gravel space as the picture below shows:

The stones are left protruding by approximately an inch and the rest are sunken in the gravel or sand depending on what your preference is. These stones have been placed with 'balance' – if they were left simply resting on top of the gravel they would be unbalanced. They have also been placed with spaces between them to encourage the garden visitor to take in all the views and elements within the garden.

As you can see the area is surrounded by shrubs and trees such as Acers and in this case gives an enclosed feel within a larger Japanese garden. The smaller you intend your garden to be will determine whether the pathway is just a visual element or not.

To build a pathway similar to this is the easiest of your options. You mark out an area, dig to a depth of 4 or 5 inches with drainage and a weed suppressant mat (more details on this when we get to a small space Zen garden) place your stones for the pathway in a layout that you feel looks good. If you don't have stones but want to get started on the planning of your Japanese garden pathway area then use plant pots or even larger potatoes to lay out your proposed stone placement – doing this will help you visualise what you are trying to achieve which is very important in the planning stage. Play around with the placements and then when you have the stones place them in each individual spot within your garden space.

Next it is time to put your gravel or sand into the garden. 8 to 10 mm gravel is probably the best size to use as it is much easier to rake and keep looking clean and tidy. Sand is another alternative but climate plays a key role in its use. In a very dry climate you can achieve much the same results as with gravel BUT if you live in a damper climate the sand will stick together like glue and make it very difficult to look tidy and raking will be almost impossible. A lesson I have learned with my Zen garden!

If you have an area of natural moss in your space you can always place the stones in this area or if you do not want sand or gravel try small pebbles instead. Remember we are looking to build a garden with a Japanese feel rather than sticking rigidly to the rules of Japanese gardening.

Another really attractive type of pathway is one that is made up of stone and stone slabs. Here is an example from Kew's Japanese garden space in London.

Lined by oriental grasses and shrubs the pathway is straight and not surrounded by gravel or sand. It IS a pathway in the strictest sense of the word and is constructed using a concrete base and the precise placement of the stone and slabs to give the pattern that you can see. Obviously this type of pathway is much more complicated but your garden space should match your vision and ambition.

There is no doubt that a path way like this will be more time consuming to build and more costly but its attractions are obvious. Be warned it is a big job and you will probably need to enlist the help of a professional.

Always try and use natural stone – sandstone and granite are the most popular and if you have an area where there is something to look at within your garden space place a larger stones area to stand on and take in the view. Your path way should look natural!

Tim recently designed a Japanese garden area from scratch for a client and you can see how he has used a solid pathway incorporating steps to a definite finishing area for the path which is where the bench is, making great use of a natural terrace that existed in the garden before it turned Japanese. Remember a pathway always has a beginning and end.

2) BRIDGES

Japanese bridges are instantly recognisable. They are an iconic image of a Japanese garden but they come in different shapes and sizes. Some are considered part of the journey through a garden and others are for stopping and taking in the view.

The two most recognisable bridges in a Japanese garden, whether arched of flat, are made of wood or stone. Bridges can be large or small which is good news as they can fit any size of Japanese garden space. A wooden arched bridge is known as a *sori bashi* and stone ones are called *sori ishibashi*. The pronounced wooden high arched bridges known as *full moon bridges* are based on original Chinese designs.

There is no easy way around a wooden bridge. They are built by skilled craftsmen and are costly in comparison to the idea we are about to show you. A wooden bridge has to be bought whole and placed within your garden in a very specific area.

There are compromises that you could consider such as laying wooden logs parallel to one another across your water area supported at either end by large stones. They need to be supported underneath by a wooden structure.

Stone bridges are the natural option and they can be flat or slightly arched. They are made of granite which is hard and durable but you could consider and option like sandstone. Your decision on what stone to use should be based on whether you intend to actually use it! Stone bridges tend to be made of uncut stone and will perhaps be one of the biggest financial outlays that you will make in your garden. Stone is not cheap but its inclusion in the form of a bridge makes it all worthwhile.

Here is an example of a stone bridge crossing a dry water body and the look is stunning and easy for you to do on a much smaller scale and at less cost.

Here's another way on having a wooden bridge on a small scale in a limited space Japanese garden area:

The bridge looks rustic and of a certain age and spans an area of water which is signified by pebbles with a stone pathway either side extending over a gravel dry water space – the bridge is part of the journey through the garden whether done physically or simply with the eye.

3) WATER FEATURES

Whether wet or dry water is one of the most important features in many types of Japanese gardens and you have many ways of introducing this element into your garden.

Water features are very important to the Japanese and apart from the drier version in a typical Zen garden they can be Basins, Waterfalls, Streams, Ponds, Bamboo spouts etc.

Water is revered in a Japanese garden for the way it looks and sounds, it can have natural motion or be a still body of water designed to reflect aspects of the garden or the moon when it is full.

Practically all water features in a Japanese garden are inspired by nature whilst some are more practical such as basins. Streams represent the journey through life and to build one as part of a Japanese garden space is fairly complicated in terms of construction and the installation of support infrastructure such as pumps and power.

In this section we have chosen to concentrate on the simpler ways of adding water to your Japanese garden through basins, bamboo fountains and spouts and a dry water space which is symbolic but very attractive and easy to do.

Basins they are found in the vast majority of Japanese gardens from the tiniest examples through to the Tea garden where they are used for guests to cleanse their hands and face before attending the ceremony. Stone basins were introduced hundreds of years ago at temples for purification purposes.

You can have a basin that just sits in position and collects water naturally or you can have one that is placed carefully, has a pump and electric supply to help clean and move the water within the feature.

Stone basins in Japanese are called *chozubachi* and look better as they become more weathered, try placing a basin in a moist darker part of your space to get a good growth of moss. Basins are nearly always made of granite and come in a number of styles.

A simple stone dish that would look really good at the side of a small Zen garden space for example. It is a cheaper option than a full blown basin which often weigh between 25 and 30 kilos!

Another option is to locate a large stone and slightly hollow out the top to give a natural water collection area. Sometimes these are referred to a rustic style basins and you can locate them in all shapes and sizes. Look for a hard stone with a slightly smooth face but not shiny. The stone should appear hard and preferably be grey in colour, a little searching around at garden centres or stone merchants should unearth your perfect stone with a totally natural look and far less of a dent in your finances.

The Tetsubachi basin is wider at the top than it is at the bottom, here is an antique one which is the kind you can pick up often cheaper than a new basin

If you would like something taller and less wide then a *Natsume-bachi basin* would be an option. It should stand on stones and water is collected via a bamboo pipe.

A Crysanthemum stone basin is called a *Kiku bachi* in Japanese. The flower petals are visible in the carving and of all the basins that you will find in a Japanese garden this type is extremely common.

You may have visited a Japanese garden and seen a round thick basin that looks like it is shaped like a coin. This type of basin is called in Japanese a *Zenigata misubachi* .

As you can see this example has a running water supply but a simpler option is to place in your garden where you feel it looks good and let natural rainfall fill the centre square cavity. The added bonus with this is climate permitting you should get some good moss growth.

Here is a simple diagram showing you how to set and provide water and power for a stone water basin this will give you the sound or running water and a really traditional feel for your dream garden space with a Japanese feel. The digging out will be the hardest work that you will have to do and the basin and the pump the most expensive acquisitions.

A word of warning bamboo in colder climates tends to split which I am sure you will agree is the last thing you want for a water pipe so hunt out a synthetic/plastic piece of piping that you can slide inside the bamboo to maintain the traditional look but prevent leakage.

Here is a diagram of what to do with your basin and how to make it operational within your garden area if you wish to have running water:

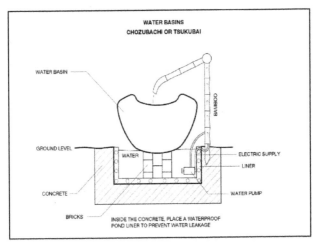

A *Tsukubai* is the name given to the area in a Tea garden where the basin and the purification area become one ahead of the Tea ceremony and this type of garden space is popular around the world because of its spiritual meaning and significance.

You will have noticed from the basin photos some really good ideas for how to present them within your garden. Plants should be chosen with big rich green leaves, ferns are perfect and at the back of the basin you can plant bigger plants and shrubs.

A larger Acer or a Japanese Maple would make a fabulous natural umbrella over the whole space but be sure to plant greenery that is good for the climate where you live and that they get the light that they need to flourish.

Bamboo spouts are another simple way of having a water ingredient in your Japanese garden space.

Here is an example of a spout or *kakei* from Kew gardens in London placed to deliver water to a large basin, this bamboo spout is open at the top and collects water naturally rather than relying on an electric pump:

To use a spout to fill a pond would require a significant pumping system and once again the best thing to do is think smaller unless space is no object. A pond can be done fairly easily if it is for ornamental purposes (not for Koi) by marking out a space, digging out the area to a depth of more than 6 inches (preferably 12inches). Kidney shapes are common as are rectangles and a far less ordered rustic shape. You can let your imagination wander!

Then seal the hole that you have excavated with hardcore and smooth concrete before placing waterproof pond liner which is also strong. This would line your hole and you can secure the sides using stakes and rocks on the ground level sides.

We have another diagram shortly that will show you how to stack rocks from the side of a pond into the central area to make your water feature natural and interesting.

A small pond will give you the water feature that you are looking for and encourage your natural creativity with its surroundings and contents. Plants and grasses on the edges with rocks will look very realistic and a spout filling the pond will give you the calming noise of running water. Placing rocks and stones around your pond and adding plantings will give you a really attractive area and adding some goldfish according to legend will bring you luck!

Tips: You will probably only need a small garden water pump it is worth checking the head height on the box to make sure your water will travel through your bamboo spout. If you live in an unpredictable climate try varnishing your bamboo to give it protection and added strength to counteract natural splitting.

Some people like a stone lantern by their water area whilst others love pond candles to induce a feeling of calmness and spirituality.

Another very simple addition is something called an *shishi odoshi* or deer scarer. This is one of the simplest additions to any Japanese garden. It is two pieces of bamboo which transfer water from top to bottom. The top piece fills with water and when it is full spills water into the lower piece which when weighted down with the water moves downwards onto a stone or rock making a rhythmic knocking sound.

You can see the first piece of bamboo coming out of the rocks and grass on the right and transferring the water to the bamboo pipe in the foreground which in turn hits the rocks to scare the deer.

Lastly, using sand or gravel to represent a body of water is a tradition that goes back hundreds of years in Japanese gardening. It is simple in a domestic Japanese garden to get the effect that you want. Later in this book you will be shown the plan and process for building a Zen style garden.

But, if you just want an area of stones, small rocks and raked gravel to plant around and prefer this feature to running water or wet water there are a number of things you can do. You can surround your area with *Azaleas, Ferns, Magnolias and Mosses.*

Maybe you would like to be ambitious and have an island within your gravel area? Perhaps you want a modern square or rectangular dry garden using gravel and pebbles?

What about simply raked gravel with some carefully placed rocks?

Here are a few examples with subtle differences:

Two spaces use gravel (pictures 1 and 2) but a different size. In picture 2 you will see a rear border area with trees and shrubs on the left hand side and a very large stone and a much smaller one in the front.

The border is the shoreline and the rocks are islands.

Picture 3 is sand that is raked with stone groupings, circular swirls around the rocks and straight raked lines travelling the length of the area.

You can have a dry water space in a large area or a much smaller area. Mark out your space if you are going for a more rustic look, plan any border to meet one edge and follow the digging out instructions in the small space Zen garden part of this book and study the diagram.

Internal spaces that suit dry water are often edged accordingly with stone and usually in square or rectangular edges and shapes. Edging is a skill that is worth learning more about to give your dry water area a very professional finish.

4) Trees, Plants and Shrubs

A Japanese garden should look older and more established than its surroundings. Plants, Shrubs and Trees can help bring your garden space to life and make it appear at one with nature. You will have to choose wisely and here are some suggestions of using plants, trees and shrubs to enhance and colour your Japanese garden area whatever type you choose to design and build.

Avoid over cluttering your garden and you may find that you have to slightly control your enthusiasm. Always pick living ingredients that suit the climate where you live and don't be afraid to plant trees like Maples in colder climates as they survive in Japan in temperatures well below minus 10 degrees.

The heat of the sun is more of an enemy than the cold and ice.

This section is going to give you some suggestions on what to consider adding to your Japanese style garden and I promise not to get too technical as this is a book on how to *simply* build a Japanese garden. As you become more adept at this form of gardening and you acquire more knowledge you can start to spread your wings a little.

A popular common element in a Japanese garden and Zen gardens are small Coniferous shrubs. Evergreens provide colour all year round and will help your other trees and plants stand out during their seasonal changes.

A good rule of thumb is for every Deciduous planting plant 2 evergreens. Coniferous shrubs really fit the bill as they are hardy and require little maintenance apart from some minor shaping and pruning. They really look striking when planted near rocks and stones and because they start off small and their appearance actually gets better over time. Remember to plant with spaces between them and other shrubs or rocks to allow this growth.

You have literally hundreds of varieties and species of Coniferous shrubs to choose from and popular varieties include *Mugo Pine*, *Dwarf Balsam firs* and *Next Spruce*.

Dwarf Balsam   **Mugo Pine**

Bamboo is another popular addition in a Japanese garden not only for separating areas but also in plant form. Tea gardens always have arrangements of Bamboo but for your small space garden then these are the varieties of Bamboo plants that will work best *sasa*, *dake*, *chiku* and *take*.

Japanese garden plants are chosen for their flowering and if you want a cavalcade of colour to contrast with your evergreens and trees then Herbaceous Japanese plants will be the solution.

Morning glory, Iris, deadnettle, Lily Turf, Kuzu Vine, White Radish, Japanese Pampas grass, Henbit, Horse Radish, Japanese Ardisia, Peony, White Chrysanthemum are plants that flower very colourfully but also in most cases have very green leaves providing a beautiful contrast.

You can use *Azaleas* and *Camellias* to great effect as well.

For the spectacular there is the climbing Japanese Wisteria which grows vertically and is covered in white flowers to a maximum height of approximately 5 feet.

Bonsai plants/trees are popular too but be warned they take quite a lot of looking after and need to be skilfully watered and pruned. These are usually placed in suitably sized pots or containers around the garden area. Some like the Japanese Maple bonsai and look wonderful planted between two rocks whilst others like Japanese Black Pine or Japanese *White Pine*, *Plum* and *Cherry* flourish better in a container.

By far the most popular bonsai plant in a Japanese garden is the *Japanese Black Pine* which is hardy and looks green all year round. A balance of colour is what you are looking to achieve throughout the 12 months of the year.

For trees it is best to start with *Acers* and *Maples* because they come in all sizes and leaf colours and they all have different autumnal colour too which will make your dream Japanese garden area so attractive in the fall or autumn.

The beautiful red colour of a Japanese Acer

I bought an Acer sapling for my garden which was about 5 inches tall and in a pot, after planting it has grown to about 18 inches in just under two years. Its leaves area deep rustic red and they shed in the autumn.

Acers/Maples come in all sorts of colours including multiple shades of green, red, orange, yellow, purple and even a light pink. If the climate is not too cold you can get multiple colours like orange, red and yellow all on one leaf! Very cold weather will give a leaf colour of deep red.

It is not just the variety of colours that make these types of trees popular because they are perfect deciduous trees for smaller gardens and love partial shade. They are slow growing and compact in form and this growth pattern can be encouraged by keeping them shady.

Dwarf varieties of Acers/Maples very rarely grow taller than six feet but this tree family does have some options if you wish to have something a little bigger. The very tallest Maples can grow up to thirty feet in height but a mid size option like a *Fireglow* Maple may be a good option as it reaches a maximum of about 11 to 12 feet when fully grown.

For small space Japanese gardens these Acers/Maples are the best to consider in your garden. *Fern leaf* or *Full Moon Maple* otherwise known as *Acer japonicum* (Aconitifolium) which in the right climate conditions will have leaves that turn all the colours of the rainbow.

Hogyoku will give you a bright orange colour in the fall whilst *Osakazuki* has a very colourful red leaf colour. *Orangeola* is a low growing tree with fairly intricate leaves and patterns. This is known as a lace leaf tree (because of their finely cut structure and likeness to lace in appearance) which typically cascade downwards from the top and with careful care and pruning can look great to the side or behind an area of rocks.

A pathway garden will also be a good home for this variety of tree. Here are some types to consider they are commonly called Disscetums: *Red dragon*, *Garnet*, *Emerald lace*, *Waterfall* and *Crimson Queen*.

Mini Maples make a really eye catching addition to any garden growing up to 15 feet in height. Pruning keeps them smaller and more compact but watch out they will spread sideways and upwards if you don't care for them. Good varieties to consider include *Glowing embers*, *Bloodgood*, *Katsura* and *Autumn glory*.

When planning your garden make sure that you will plant trees in the right place. They need some sun for the colouring of the leaves but not total sunlight which can damage the leaves and affect growth. Smaller trees like acidic soil and being surrounded by acid loving plants that are famous in Japanese gardens such as *Azaleas*, *Ferns*, *Rhododendrons* and any small ground level conifers.

Alkaline soil may be ok but the root system will need to be established from planting with heavy watering twice a week to encourage growth. If you area is too sunny leaf colour will be affected – a dark red leaf would have a much lighter colour. Too much shade and the red leaves will revert to green. This means that what you want to plant will affect the space you choose for your garden.

A general rule is the smaller the variety the more sun it can take and the green leaved types are more resistant to sun than red leafed trees. If you care for your Acers and Maples they will last for a long while maybe even generations.

Let your imagination wander as you plan your garden and watch your plants, shrubs and trees flourish to give you an authentic Japanese feel. There are hundreds of varieties for you to discover that would be at home in this type of garden but the information that I have given you will help you get started quickly as I have kept it simple.

5) Courtyard Gardens

Of all the types of domestic Japanese garden the 'Courtyard Garden' is in many ways the type that makes the best immediate visual impression. It is enclosed and nearly always in a small space within a domestic area and therefore is scrutinised by the eye more than most. This means you will have to plan it well and use the right quality ingredients to get the best result.

You do not have to have a courtyard in the middle of your property, any space that you can make with defined edges and preferably a wall can be turned into a *Tsuboniwa* (courtyard garden). A patio area that you can isolate and border would be just as good.

The Japanese introduced them into their homes to give a feeling of light and nature within a central space in the house. Occupiers would be able to see the courtyard garden from several living spaces within the home.

Originally, Japanese courtyard gardens were small micro-gardens as part of a much larger building structure. They started off being really quite small just under 4 metres square in non-metric size that is around 11 feet squared, perfect for a small garden project for you.

So what are the elements you can use when making a Japanese courtyard garden? If you wish to be accurate and traditional then a stone basin is a must, stone pathways, a lantern, maybe a small bridge and some garden stones. These are all strong elements and are often referred to by designers as 'hardscape'.

Hardscaping will help you physically map out your chosen space and your design ideas. For example you could place a small bridge (stone or wooden) over an area of sand or gravel (depicting water) or you could place a few larger stones within your design that would mimic real landscapes like mountains.

Plants, shrubs and herbaceous trees will complete the finished design. As always, my advice is to sketch out your designs before starting the construction. A scale to work to is one inch squared equals one square foot on your plan.

It is quite possible that your Japanese courtyard garden area will have a wall (s) on each side and may be denied generous sunlight so you will have to pick your trees, shrubs and plants accordingly. If it is a really shady are then go for mosses – they will flourish and provide a blanket of different greens and the occasionally light brown to accentuate your hardscape features.

Here is a a very interesting courtyard garden taking up a fairly large space but notice how the dwarf trees are placed and really stand out in contrast to the wooden floor.

Your sunlight in the garden will dictate what plants and shrubs will flourish in an area of direct sunlight, shade or bright light (not direct sunlight).It is a small scale garden so try and stick with dwarf bonsai and a good dollop of groundcover plants that fit your environment. Always check the growing needs before buying to avoid disappointment.

The chances are your Japanese courtyard garden will not be blessed with lots of natural water so pick plants that require little water. If you feel uncomfortable about including plants, shrubs and bonsai trees then you can always just design a space that is a traditional '*Tsuboniwa*'. By this I mean DRY – no water or plants etc. The earliest and more traditional courtyard gardens follow this 'rule'.

They used rocks, sand and gravel to copy real landscapes scenes from a familiar local area. It is fun using your imagination – rake sand in swirls to signify water, a stone basin containing water can signify a lake or even an ocean! White or light sand has the added benefit of bringing reflective light into a darker space. You can choose to go small medium or large with your landscape copying, it will depend on the size of your available area.

A Japanese courtyard garden takes some organisation and thought. Don't just place ingredients willy nilly. Your plan should reflect an area of contemplation, tranquillity and spiritual learning and reflection. Do not overcrowd it! But make it look as though it functions as part of your daily life adding balance to your home.

I heard a saying that is SO true …."Plan your Japanese courtyard garden with a minimalist approach and the economy of a poet"

Courtyard garden design ideas and tips:

Ring a dry pond area with roof tiles placed on their side and place your gravel inside, leaving a protruding inch or two of the tile to provide a recognizable edge to the water.

Use sand and gravel plus stones which are often rectangular in shape. A banana shaped stone is fairly common in courtyard gardens.

Bamboo screens allow somebody to look into the garden but a cover to a window.

Courtyard gardens have an entrance like nearly all Japanese gardens and a stepping stone small path to a lantern or basin surrounded by green plants is a very attractive way of laying out this type of garden. Remember when planning your garden consider how it will look in each season.

Drainage is important if your courtyard garden is exposed to the elements. A normal way of doing this is having a drainage outlet for water and covering it with small stones which disguise the drain and allow water to simply trickle through the gaps and away from the garden. This is the only part of a potential project that will need professional help for laying a drainage pipe from your drainage area.

If you have a larger space for a courtyard garden a bamboo fence is a really attractive way of setting out the boundaries helped by plants, shrubs and trees.

Sprinkle water over the garden if it is dry before guests arrive – this shows off the garden in all its glory and is a tradition in Japan.

Little leaf box shrubs, Azaleas, Japanese acuba, smaller

Maples, Sasanqua (green and white leaves), Sasa veitchi, Ferns, Forsythia in pots, Chrysanthemums and Moss make very good to add to the garden and some give lovely ground cover.

Frame a lantern with shrubs like Japanese cypress. I once saw this in a courtyard garden and it looked so authentic and beautiful. Place your Japanese lantern where you want it to be and behind it plant taller growing plants or trees. At the front place low level shrubs and at the sides plants and shrubs that grow to a good height that you can prune and shape.

When the plants and shrubs have grown sufficiently you will see that you lantern is framed in the middle of an evergreen area and the main part of the lantern will be visible rather like a picture on a television screen. Really effective and typically Japanese.

6) Tree and Water Gardens

These types of Japanese gardens can be hugely ambitious or smaller in scale than perhaps you imagine. They consist of more than trees and water but they are the two principle elements. I like to think of this type of garden as a bit of a blank canvass.

Trees and water open up the garden when being viewed as they grow vertically and outwards providing depth and a natural look. You can add rocks and stones plus a lantern and plenty of shrubs and plants that should be chosen to reflect the seasons. This is true of the trees in the garden as well.

All plantings are done in a natural way so you would not see carefully and heavily pruned and shaped shrubs as in other Japanese gardens. Pruning in this type of garden is done to show off the natural character of the trees and plants.

Water provides the sound of the garden as do the trees when they sway gently in the breeze. Ideally you would build a stream or a pond (unless you are lucky enough to have one already!) and it is important to understand that the body of water is there to reflect the life of the garden and as a result of this 'rule' a designer would think long and hard about where the water should be situated.

A tree and water garden with a pond –you can see the reflection –stones, low level planting and larger tree.

In my bid to keep things simple for you and your garden if the thought of a pond is something that you find daunting or consider too expensive the easier option is to revert to a dry water space of gravel or white sand. This will add another dimension to the original principles of a tree and water garden and make life a little easier too.

Apart from the two principle ingredients large and small stones are added and their natural look within the garden is magnified by growing low level shrubs and small plants between them allowing the growth to partially cover some of the stones and rocks natural surfaces.

If you would like a stream with running water there is an obvious cost for a pump, liner and the elements that will make a stream look natural. Things like small stones or pebbles intermingled with larger stones that tend to be direction markers for the way that a person's eye journeys through the garden.

A dry tree and water garden with traditional wooden flat bridge, stones, rocks, trees, shrubs and a shoreline near the main entrance – something that you could do on a smaller scale.

By this I mean, small stones should be placed carefully and then set within the ground in such a way that they lead the eye along the stream showing off what is either side and at the end in the form of trees and shrubbery and hopefully seasonal colours.

You can fairly easily construct a much smaller scale tree and water garden. In your body of water whether wet or dry submerge 4 or 5 large stones ensuring that approximately half of the stone is laid underwater or within your sand or gravel.

Place the stones as a slightly offset line of rocks with a reasonable gap between them and on one of the stones cultivate some moss or grass and plant a small pine tree or similar. The small tree on one rock will give the appearance of a large body of water like an ocean with the small tree on a rock putting the garden in proportion. Once again some imagination is needed to get the best results.

You should be able to see a balance in the gardens design from whichever angle you view it from as should a visitor.

Japanese gardens should have the simplest materials and this is why with the knowledge that you are hopefully getting from this book means creating one inexpensively with fantastic results and relatively low maintenance is something you should be confident of achieving.

Never be afraid of an empty space in any type of Japanese garden because they will show off and compliment the other elements in your garden. Less really is more.

7) BAMBOO

There are thousands of different varieties of bamboo and they are a really natural ingredient in many types of Japanese gardens. Because they are quite virulent in their growth you can get results quickly and make good use in smaller gardens of Dwarf bamboo.

One of the finest collections of bamboo outside Japan is at Kew gardens in London and the area is carefully looked after by Ken Townshend and his team. The bamboo area at Kew contains a Minka house, one of the most traditional family homes in the 18th and 19th century. There are over 1200 different types of bamboo in the garden surrounding the house and specimens range from the small-leafed *Fargesia nitida* to the variegated *Arundinaria fortunei*.

Bamboos are members of the grass family. They actually are perennial plants and part of the *Poaceae* family (grasses). They range from dwarf species that rarely exceed 0.5 metres tall to giant varieties that grow as high as 35 metres with timber bamboo growing at the rate of a metre a day. Because they can tolerate climates from cold mountain regions to warm, tropical areas there will be many types of bamboo for your garden area.

The Minka House at Kew gardens in London. Bushes of the sacred bamboo *(Nandina domestica* 'firepower') are planted around the entrances.This plant, which has brilliant yellow, orange and red leaves, is alleged to dispel bad dreams.

Bamboo plants are hardy and don't need a lot of help to flourish as they require no pesticides or fertilizers to grow and need little water. In extreme weather whether it be dry or flooding they will struggle and need a little help just like any other plant.

Bamboo is popular because it makes fantastic ornamental focal points, privacy screens, hedging, windbreaks, ground cover, and landscape design features in the domestic garden. At the beginning of this book I mentioned that you will need a quiet space to have your Japanese style garden but if you are struggling to find a noise free spot then live fast growing bamboo will provide a noticeable noise screen for your garden with the added bonus a making its own calming sound in the wind!

If you are looking for an ornamental bamboo plant for a focal point in your garden and have a certain area of space to allocate to this as a structural planting, be sure to choose a 'clumping' bamboo.

If on the other hand you are planning on planting for a windbreak or privacy screen of bamboo, a running species will fill that up nicely but you will need to put a barrier in place to make sure it only grows where you want it to. At Kew they used plastic barriers to curb the growth of enthusiastic bamboo.

If you live in a colder climate and have harsh winters you will need to choose a types of bamboo that can tolerate cold temperatures and freezing through ice and snow. Choosing the wrong type of bamboo for your garden will cost you time, money and effort.

This means when you visit a nursery or garden centre ensure that you read the label and look for the temperature tolerance of the plant, if you are in any doubt ask for help. The placement of your garden will determine its temperature. On a hill it will be colder, it will be the same if it is north facing and naturally warmer if south facing, be sure to give yourself some temperature leeway when buying bamboo.

For example, if your lowest recorded temperature is -10 centigrade then perhaps buy a bamboo plant that can survive in temperature of -5 centigrade rather than pushing a species to the limit as you will want it to start well in the next growing season.

You can protect your bamboo by placing the ground around the bottom with a mulch such as tree bark or leaves this will ensure that the roots and rhizomes are protected for good growth.

Tip: bamboo plants in the ground survive more than those planted in pots because as it is lower to the ground. Make sure that you buy bamboo well before the winter and give its root system adequate time to get established in your garden.

Several clumping bamboos set at certain distances apart will make an equally effective windbreak or hedge but will grow in clumps rather than spread by sending rhizome runners underground. Snow weighs bamboo down so you will need to remove it by gently shaking the bamboo and remember a cold wind can do just as much damage so protect your bamboo in cold snaps.

Dwarf bamboo makes an excellent ground cover within a Japanese garden, not only do they look nice as focal points alongside water , stones and rocks but they also protect the ground from the sun helping your garden to maintain good moisture levels. Importantly dwarf bamboo does not spread so quickly making it easier to maintain and control.

Aim to use bamboo plants that are less than 2 to 3 feet in height and if you want a larger bamboo of 10 feet or above this would be used for shading in your Japanese garden area. You may be wondering what types of dwarf bamboo are the best to use and I have picked 3 types for you to consider for your garden plans:

Pleioblastus distichus 'Mini' – a really good ornamental ground cover with pretty aggressive and rapid spreading - Maximum height: 1' - Maximum diameter: 0 1/8".

Pleioblastus viridistriatus chrysophyllus – This is an excellent ground cover plant but also makes a good container plant. It spreads aggressively and can even be used for hedging. It has golden yellow leaves with lighter green stripes approximately 7" by 1 1/2" - Maximum height: 3' - Maximum diameter: 1/4".

Pleioblastus viridistriatus or **Dwarf Greenstripe** - Attractive dwarf bamboo that is fabulous ground cover and a useable container plant once again with aggressive spreading – once again it also makes good hedging – with golden yellow leaves with green stripes in spring approximately 7" by 1 1/2" –

You can mow it in winter - Maximum height: 3' - Maximum diameter: 1/4".

Your options with bamboo in a Japanese garden are plentiful but one of the most popular uses of bamboo within a garden space is as a boundary with fencing being a very common feature.

If you are ambitious and keen to make a realistic representation of a Japanese garden then a couple of things you will be probably be interested in are gates and fencing.

Most Japanese gardens are intended to be seen from outside looking in and should have a feeling of being separate from our everyday world. Enclosure of the garden is achieved by the use of gates and fences often made of Bamboo.

Zen gardens are tranquil and for contemplation whilst a Japanese garden is also a place where visitors can go to escape from the stresses and strains of life – a gate signifies the place where you can enter this separate world and a signifier of returning to the world outside once you exit the garden.

You may think that fences are all about 'enclosure' and that thought would seem obvious and to a certain extent is right. Fences also have another meaning associated with them and it's called *Miegakure* which in Japanese translates roughly as 'Hide and reveal'.

So if you are thinking of making a Japanese garden imagine how visually tantalising some bamboo fencing would be adorned with climbers that give the visitor a small glimpse of what lies behind your fencing – a stunning Japanese garden space. There are a lot of different designs and construction methods used in bamboo fencing and there will be one for your garden however simple or complicated it may be.

The whole concept of using gates and fences in a Japanese garden is all about teasing what lies within the boundaries and containing the space for respite from everyday life with definable borders for garden privacy. This is one of the main reasons people living outside of Japan are interested in using bamboo either in its wildest form of as a constructed boundary.

A Japanese garden is a miniature expression of nature and should if possible be sealed off from the outside world and its worth remembering that fences and even gates are just as important in a Japanese garden as a stone lantern or Azaleas!

8) FLAT GARDEN

Flat gardens or *Hira-niwa* in Japanese are an extension on the Zen style garden that you are familiar with. They depict a seaside area or a large lake and have several ingredients for you to be inspired by.

There is always a flat area with gravel or coarse sand which is raked to give the illusion of the movement of water. Sometimes a flat garden area can be made up of small pebbles which is an interesting take that is worth thinking about for your garden area.

In a flat garden you will also find stones, trees and shrubs , a stone lantern which illuminates the garden at night and a well for the purification of the viewer and visitor. If you do not want a water feature then consider upright oblong stones that can signify a waterfall of the dry variety!

This type of Japanese garden came to the fore in the *Edo* period and because of the visually depth and simplicity were seen as larger objects of contemplation

To be clear a *karesansui* garden is a typical Zen style garden with an area of dry water and minimal number of carefully chosen rocks or stones to represent a landscape whether existing or imaginary.

A flat garden takes this original design to the next level as you can see in the picture below with shrubs of depth and shaping on the edges gives the garden visual depth and space.

The gravel is the water and the mountains on the shoreline are depicted by the rounded shapes of shrubs like azaleas.

A flat garden is meant to be viewed from one area and because of their design should appear framed to the eye in much the same way that you would look at a landscape painting. They do not make ideal small Japanese gardens but if you are feeling ambitious a medium size garden would be perfect.

As in any Japanese garden planting is important to reflect the changing seasons and by using Maples and their autumnal colours your garden would look stunning in the fall. Cherry trees are a good idea for beautiful colours in the spring. Japanese black pines look best in winter and for summer you have the imaginary raked gravel cool sea.

Rocks are placed in the gravel to represent enlightenment and happiness.

You could do as many ingredients as you wish and perhaps introduce carefully laid stepping stones across the gravel area instead of placing rocks in the garden. The shoreline is what will make this garden and the plants and shrubs suggested will help you define the seasons and make a visually stunning example of a flat garden.

The method for successfully making a gravel area with good drainage (which is essential) is explained in the small space Zen garden section of this book. Flat gardens require more work and planning but make one of the most memorable types of Japanese garden for the visitor and owner.

9) Stones and Rocks

Once again I am going to keep this section simple. The significance of their meaning and use in Japanese gardens is huge. Japanese gardeners and designers think very carefully about what type they use and where they are situated in a garden.

Kyoto is home to some of the world's most famous and recognisable rock gardens and their style is copied all over the world. To the purists the placement of stones and rocks is a very exact science. For example, at Kew gardens in London the dry landscape section of their impressive Japanese garden area is visited regularly by the designer from Kyoto simply to check that the angles of the placement of the stones is correct. If they have moved even fractionally then they are moved back to the angle of resting that they are intended to be in.

As ever I would like to give you a little background knowledge first which will help you if you are keen to have an accurate representation of the use of stones and rocks in your Japanese garden.

The use of stones and rocks in a Japanese gardens or Zen gardens is an essential element in their design. The rules governing their usage are ancient and plentiful, what I plan to do in this section is give you an overview of the types of rocks and stones used together with some basic rules of design.

Stones and rocks are symbolic representations of real or mythical land forms. The first stone grouping to be introduced into Japanese gardens was the *Shumisen–* a collection of stones, where the Buddha lives in the main central stone and his disciples are the smaller stones around the Buddha.

Chinese legend and in particular the *Isles of Eternal youth* made an impact in Japanese gardens in the Heian era approximately 781 to 1185 AD. These taller stones made up the group of islands which represent the unattainable dwelling place of the Immortals. It is depicted by one larger stone is surrounded by 3 smaller ones. This is a typical example of a Chinese influence in the use of Japanese garden rocks and stones.

There are 5 main types of stone groupings in a Japanese rock garden and each type has a name and a meaning. These stones and rocks can be used in many combinations so if you are thinking of designing your own Japanese rock garden or adding to what you already have there is plenty of scope for creativity!

The first type of stone is the *Soul Stone* it is low and vertical.

Secondly, is the *Body Stone* which is as a rule tall and vertical. The third type of stone is called *The Heart Stone* or *Flat Stone* and that's exactly what it is. Fourthly, is the *Branching Stone* or Arching stone and last but not least is the *Ox Stone* which can also be known as the 'reclining' stone.

All of these stones are included in Japanese rock gardens and Japanese gardens because of their 'positive' meaning and influence but, as you know in life for every positive there is usually a negative and so it is in Japanese gardens.

Bad stones and rocks can be put into 3 categories and these are never used in Japanese rock gardens. Firstly, there are *Diseased Stones* these are stones that are withered or have a misshapen top. Secondly, comes the *Dead Stone* this is a stone that is obviously used as a horizontal one and vice versa and finally, the *Pauper Stone* which is a stone that has no direct connection in terms of shape, size or composition to any other stones in the garden.

Don't worry we are not going to get caught up in such technicalities but I thought it important to give you a sense of their importance.

Stones and rocks add to the meaning and balance of a Japanese garden and their quality is judges by colour ,shape ,texture and in some cases the original location of the rock. Sought after stones and rocks have been known to have been sold for hundreds of thousands of dollars but for our purposes our budget is a lot smaller.

To see an imposing single vertical stone standing in a sea of gravel is a simple statement and one that you could do very easily. Surround the gravel area with shrubs and the singularity of the stone makes the garden unique and memorable. You do not need a great deal of space to do this either.

In Japan rocks gardens are sometimes found in bathrooms so an internal small garden is a real option for you. Rocks should be placed simply with balance as you can see in the diagram below and I have included a demonstration of how to use rocks around a water feature too. The bank of the water feature is covered and hidden by supported rocks under and in the water which is a really nice visual touch for a garden ingredient.

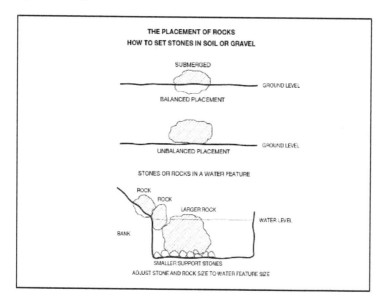

The calming effect and spiritual significance of stone and rock in a Japanese garden is something a lot of people desire. Place yours where you feel they visually please the eye within the concept of you space.

Use a single stone or an odd number for stone groupings that will tie your garden to nature. The most common types of stone used in a Japanese garden are granite, sandstone, andesite, basalt, limestone and chlorite and stone merchants and garden centres will be able to supply these for you unless you already have some stones that you have set aside to use. Avoid straight hard edges and aim for slightly smoother stones that are more rounded which represent energy, elegance and refinement.

Plants and shrubs can be grown on the sides of your rock garden and you already have enough ideas for what to plant but for a totally natural look moss growth on placed stones is the icing on the cake for a Japanese garden. This depends wholly on the dampness of your climate for successful moss growth.

The placement of your stones should tempt and draw in the eye in a focused direction and when you use them your garden will be tied to nature giving the impression of natural landscapes of mountains and cliffs surrounded by foliage.

A Simpler alternative would be to build a simple sea of pebbles with some rocks and low level shrubs and add an ornament like a basin or lantern which are available in all shapes and sizes. Bamboo and oriental grasses could skirt the sea area giving your small garden a very authentic feel. Pebbles and gravel come in all colours and shapes and sizes meaning that you can have a chunkier look or a fine look for your garden.

Pebbles and slate can be used when carefully placed to simulate running water as in this garden design:

You could have a rectangular dry gravel space with a single large rock and 3 separate ones in a grouping and surround the rectangle with slightly raised wooden decking where a pot plant or bonsai in a traditional dish would not look out of place.

For a courtyard style garden an idea maybe for an enclosed dry water area with 3 rocks and much taller bamboo planted deliberately protruding out from the gravel. Beautifully simple and very low maintenance.

Stones not only represent land mass but also things like ships in the ocean and for a craggy hillside effect use stones and rocks with abstract shapes. If you have a slight upslope of a few feet in your garden maybe consider building support terracing and place large natural stones at the top and smaller in proportion different stones on the way down the terracing. Fill the gaps between the stones and rocks with pebbles or gravel to create the illusion of running water down a hillside.

Stones and rocks will make your Japanese garden area complete and their importance within this art from should never be underestimated. You will have a lot of fun sketching your design, finding your stones, setting them within your plan and seeing the simple results make your Japanese garden come to life.

Tips:

Try and use uncut stones that show signs of weathering.

If you wish to have more than 2 stones or rocks in your garden the normal arrangement for larger numbers is in groups of 3,5 and 7.

Try and capture the variety of the rocks ensuring different sizes and shapes are next to each other. You do not want a uniform look as a Japanese garden shows nature despite the interference of man and should look that way.

Remember to set your stones in sand or gravel to a depth of a few inches to achieve a realistic result.

If you want a rock garden with plantings make sure that you water them well in summertime as the heat of the sun on the rocks and stones in your garden is very powerful and is easily transferred and damaging to low level shrubs.

10) A Zen garden (in a Small space)

This type of garden had always appealed to me and earlier in this book I showed you the before and after of my small space Japanese Zen garden. I love the simplicity of the look and how when you get started with a basic one such as mine you can add areas and ingredients as you get more confident and knowledgeable.

I came up with a plan on how I wanted it to look and rather than show you my poor quality artwork, for the purpose of this part of the book I got somebody to draw up a simple plan that is easy to follow. It shows the area, the ingredients, the dimensions, land differences, plantings, edging and stone layout.

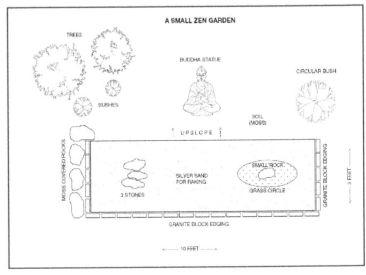

The amount of space needed for this is small and I have placed my garden at the foot of an upslope and intend to add more low level plantings at the bottom and behind the Buddha statue add a bamboo screen. I suppose my design is a Zen hill and pond garden a derivative of several styles and that is an important point for you to understand.

Make whatever style (s) of Japanese style garden you wish after all it is your garden idea and you have freewill!

Let me take you through the exact process of how my small space Zen garden was built and it is something that this spring I will be adding to by planting Irises, introducing a new space to encompass 2 beautiful dwarf crab apple trees that I have which flower pink and deep red in the spring along with a new rock grouping and a dry riverbed.

STEP 1. Take a look at the various possible areas where you feel you could locate your Zen garden. Consider the positive and negative aspects of each spot.

You will need a quite area with little noise pollution from neighbours or busy roads. For my Zen garden I chose an area of my rear garden/yard that was secluded and had enough space to complement its surroundings and be aesthetically pleasing to look at once built.

STEP 2. It is really helpful to sketch out a plan for your garden idea in scale on a piece of paper. Nothing too fancy just lay out the dimensions and how you expect it to look in terms of size, edges, plants, trees, stones and rocks etc. A good scale to use is 1 inch to 1 foot or 2.5cm to 1 square metre, of course you can make the scale bigger if you wish.

You will have seen from my plan that I had a very clear idea of the layout and what it would look like after construction. The beauty of planning on a piece of paper means that you can alter your plan easily as the mood takes you.

My space marked out and with stones in place

STEP 3. You need to then dig out the area to a depth of 4 to 6 inches and as you can see above although the sides are not perfectly straight they will be in the finished garden. When digging out try to ensure that you remove any obstacles like pieces of stone and weeds or they will come back to haunt you and your garden in the future.

Do spend some time doing this as it will get you the best results. Spray the dug-out cleared area with a very strong weed killer when you have a space ready. You may be lucky and because of where you live and the space you have available it may not be as difficult as it was for me – shale infested soil with small rocks and made up predominantly of clay are a bit of a back breaker!

STEP 4. Next, it's the `EDGING´ that needs to be done. Edging comes in multiple varieties. It can be wooden planks, stone slabs or in my case small blocks of a type of granite called ´Storm´ these types of edging blocks are available from any garden centre or Home depot as well as specialist aggregate suppliers all over the world.

Granite edging blocks laid in a straight line and set in concrete

You need to measure the exactly lengths of the sides of your garden and work out how much edging you will need. For my garden the cost of the blocks was around 80 Pounds Sterling or approx. 110 US Dollars. Brush your edging before setting in concrete to get rid of any impurity; you are ready to position it around the garden area.

Be generous with your concrete as it has to hold the edging and within the garden quite a weight of sand or gravel. Tip: do NOT attempt to concrete edging if rain is in the weather forecast as it will struggle to set and you will have to go back to square one. Try and wait for a couple of dry days for the best results.

STEP 5. This involves completing all of the edging and pointing the granite blocks with concrete. Cement is carefully inserted in between each block and you would use this exact same method if you were working with lengthier blocks of stone or larger slabs.

The cement has to be stronger than that used for brickwork in a house which has a tendency to crumble over time when exposed to the elements. This process is time consuming and when you have finished you will see the shape of your garden really coming to life.

Place your weed suppressant mat within the confines on the pointed garden blocks and get as tight to them as you can. This type of matting comes in rolls and I had plenty left over for my next project! The cost of the matting was around £35.00 or 50 USD.

Double check that the mat has a snug fit and pierce the bottom liberally with holes to aid drainage from you garden. This part of the construction is not for short cuts and the extra effort put in to do it correctly will ensure future rewards.

STEP 6. I opted for just stones in my Zen garden and the single stone on its own in the nearly completed project will be surrounded by a grass island land mass which I know will look superb against the silver sand. My Buddha statue, stone basin, bamboo screen and a small *acer* tree will go on the upward slope behind the Zen area.

I got my stones from a local merchant and chose naturally smooth stones for my garden. However at the sides on the left I have the contrast of larger granite stones covered in moss. I did not buy the stones online and I recommend that you don't either. Take a trip and look at various types so that you pick the right ones for the plan you have in your mind's eye.

Stones and rocks of certain shapes and sizes will naturally attract you whilst others won't so go with your gut feeling. When you have them lay them out on your mat in the position that you want them and you can either cut a hole in the mat that mirrors the bottom of the stone if you are confident that you have suppressed any weeds or you can leave them where you have placed them and get ready to add your sand or gravel. The stones that I used in the garden cost around £45 or 60 USD.

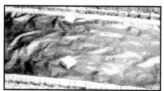

A snug fit my mat – very important!

STEP 7. Sand or Gravel? I opted wrongly for Silver sand and it is something I am in the process of rectifying. Sand does not like lots of water as it sticks to together and apart from in dry spells is difficult to rake correctly. I really recommend that you choose gravel and of a size of 8-10mm as drainage is good and raking is far simpler.

I used a metric tonne of sand and it cost around £85 or 110 USD so not overly expensive. Gravel would be slightly more expensive but the results would be better. The mat and the stones were in place so the sand was poured in around the stones setting them within the area for balance and to achieve the correct look. They rest on the mat so are 4 to 5 inches in depth covered by the sand.

At the other side of the edges I placed larger gravel chunks and some additional soil on the foot of the upslope to ready for additional low level plants and shrubs which I want to edge the rear of the garden as you look at it.

Here it is today before the sand removal.

So you can see that the process is not difficult and with allowing concrete to dry and source everything I had my garden 80 per cent complete in about 10 days. As the spring approaches I will add gravel to where the sand is and extending my Japanese garden area all of which will be covered in my free Japanese garden newsletter **The Japanese Garden Bulletin.**

I would love you to get involved and as you have a love of Japanese gardens you will be blown away what I have got lined up for you – articles, pictures, designs, interviews, video's on Japanese gardens with some of the top experts in the world!

And finally …..

11) A Complete Domestic Japanese Garden Project By Tim Sykes

Tim was asked by a family in Tunbridge Wells in England to dramatically change their garden into one with a Japanese style. Tim considered the natural layout and features of the garden and went about designing and building a very impressive space.

Here in Tim's own words and pictures he takes you through the project and hopefully it will inspire you to start your own dream garden space with a touch of Japan.

A Japanese Oasis

by Tim Sykes of Gardenproud

©Gardenproud 2013

If you are contemplating a tranquil space to relax then think Japanese!

A Japanese style garden can deliver a kaleidoscope of colour with strong focal points throughout the year.

For the ruling elite Japanese gardens were created as sanctuaries where emperors could escape from the day to day hustle and bustle of life or periods of strife and conflict that marked Japan's history.

The character of many of the more well-known Japanese Gardens of today owe much to the influence of Zen Buddhism imported from China hundreds of years ago.

Many Japanese gardens embody different garden styles or compartments, which combine to create a sense of wellbeing and tranquillity. Typically they include a Natural Garden, a Tea Garden, a sand and stone garden, a Strolling Pond or Water Garden and a Flat Garden.

Earlier last year we were fortunate enough to be invited to create an oriental style garden in the centre of Tunbridge Wells, Kent, United Kingdom.

Our client had a steeply sloping terraced garden that had been neglected. He wanted a relatively low maintenance garden, with strong focal points, a seating area, a place to entertain (drink tea with his friends), and a larger terrace closer to the house.

The garden already benefited from two rather beautiful and well-established Acer trees, and a large Rhododendron bush. There were a number of rocks supporting paved areas collapsing amongst the undergrowth. At the top of the garden sat a rusty old garden bench surrounded by a sea of tall grass.

Despite the condition of the garden we could see the potential and these few clues set a train of thought, which led to our eventual solution.

We decided that we wanted to create a garden that was influenced by Japanese styles, but our interpretation rather than following any strict guidelines.

Our vision for the garden was inspired by those at Chinzan-so, in Tokyo, and the Japanese Gardens in Portland, Oregon.

"I adore the combination of colours and focal points that adorn Japanese gardens in particular the use of red(my favourite colour) that often highlights a bridge, or pergola, or tea house."

Our design incorporated terraces, the use if rocks, trees and architectural plants to help create a series of focal points in an asymmetrical layout that takes your eye on a journey through the garden, culminating in a bright red bench sitting at its peak.

"To draw the eye and as a real feature we designed the new garden to incorporate a gloss red Lutyens bench set against a backdrop of a similarly crafted dense green hedge."

A winding irregular sandstone rock staircase connects a series of terraces and rockeries, each featuring a new planting concept, with linking themes using a pallette of colour - pinks, reds, purples and lilacs.

Rustic posts and handrails juxtapositioned on either side of each flight of steps provide practical assistance to the elderly visitors and further help direct the eye.

A planting plan was created that would help emphasise the Japanese theme and included Tree Ferns, Grasses, Acers of contrasting colours, Camelias, Phormiums, Buxus Balls, Azaleas, Rhododendrons, Magnolias .

Many tons of new Sandstone Rocks were brought in to create new rockery walls and new flights of steps. The use of Indian Sandstone pavers has been augmented with interesting stone patterns to create new features.

A large circular mid terrace has been created for a table and chairs to be situated in the shade of a large rhododendron where afternoon tea can be enjoyed.

Further steps then lead down to a lower patio area and the house.

Finally, trellising helps to camouflage an otherwise unattractive shed and unify the design of the lower terrace.

This book has been put together to inspire you and perhaps more importantly to get you excited about turning part of your yard or garden into a Japanese space.

Whether small, medium or large I hope we have given you the tools to design and build a Japanese style garden with confidence and we would love to see photos and video of your efforts.

Japanese gardens give you a chance to be at one with nature and to reproduce its beauty as well as create a space that has been touched by a human hand but looks so natural and established that no one would ever believe it!

You have all the tools and ingredient information that you need to make your dream garden a reality. If you have any questions we are always very happy to hear from you and try and help.

Good luck!

Copyright © Zenibo Marketing Ltd 2013

www.ingramcontent.com/pod-product-compliance
Lightning Source LLC
Chambersburg PA
CBHW071728141224
19009CB00032B/903